ALISDAIR MARSHALL'S

Scottish Murder Stories

G SYNE PUBLISHERS LTD.

INTRODUCTION

Every time the second hand of your watch sweeps round — someone, somewhere, is murdered.

In some countries there are so many killings, that murder accounts for more deaths than disease. We, in Scotland, are comparatively lucky. As yet there is no indication that the violence in the backstreet ghettos of cities like Detroit, Dallas and New York, will spread to our larger cities. Thankfully, life to most of us, is still sacroscant.

Scotland, none the less, would still be well-represented in any pecking order of homicide. You might say, if you were of macabre bent, that what we lack in quantity, we make up for in quality. For when a Scot decides to kill, he tends to do it with some style.

The scenic grandeur of Scotland has sometimes provided a beautiful and incongruous backcloth for sinister and ugly deeds. Was the macabre death of Netta Farnario on the Holy Isle of Iona, really a "psychic killing?" Whose were the severed limbs in "The Devil's Beeftub?" Who died on the summit of Arran's "Mountain of the Winds?" What were the Hopetoun Quarry Scarecrows?

Beneath the sober, Calvinistic exterior, dark passions sometimes burned, which eventually erupted in murderous violence. What went into Dr.Cream's "pink pills for pale prostitutes?" Why did the douce Aberdeen housewife kill her neighbour's bairn? What turned the Glasgow Sunday-school teacher into an assassin?

In the realms of detection too, we were never laggard. Our pathologists, notably, Sydney Smith, Harvey Littlejohn and the professors Glaister, father and son, were second to none. The case of the murderous Pole who struck down an innocent gamekeeper's wife . . .the bloody jigsaw of Gardenholme Linn . . .the sack murder in the Granite City . . .the trail that led to the Beast of Broxburn. All are now established as "classics" in medico/criminal circles around the world, while the crimes themselves are firmly esconced in murder's Hall of Fame.

"Scottish Murder Stories".
Published by Lang Syne Publishers Ltd.,
45 Finnieston Street, Glasgow G3 8JU.
Tel: 0141-204 3104
Printed by Dave Barr Print,
45 Finnieston Street, Glasgow G3 8JU.
Tel: 0141-221 2598

First published 1983. Reprinted 1984, 1985, 1986, 1987, 1988, 1989, 1990 and 1995.

ISBN No. 0 946264 47 3

Death in the Gully of Fire

The heather blazed purple in the midsummer sun as two young men sprawled on the summit of Goatfell — the 3000ft "mountain of the winds" on Arran.

It was a holiday idyll on an enchanted island. But it was an idyll that was to end in horrific death for one young man and 41 years rotting behind prison bars for the other.

As the sun lowered in the west and the brassy heat diminished, the two climbers prepared for their descent. To other holiday acquaintances they appeared well matched . . .one an extrovert, chatterbox from London, the other a taciturn Scot from Glasgow. But deep in the flawed mind of John Watson Laurie, a £2-a-week pattern maker, a murderous resentment stirred.

Why should Edwin Robert Rose, this upstart clerk from the South, be better-off than he? Would his incessant prattle and boasting about money and success never end?

The expensive gold watch and chain on Rose's waistcoat winked mockingly in the sun. As they descended the steep, treacherous, rock face, with the Londoner in the lead, the fine tweed of his hand-made suit and jaunty cap was a constant goad. The ensemble was the kind of status symbol Laurie had always longed for but had never been able to afford. It should be his by right.

A murderous surge of rage and envy swept through him. Without pausing or breaking his stride, he stooped to clasp a jagged granite boulder. In the same movement he swung at the expensive tweed of the jaunty cap with all the pent up fury of his bottled resentment.

The shock of the blow staggered Rose. The hated cap sailed over the sheer precipice on his right. Mute with disbelief, his eyes locked, uncomprehending, with Laurie's for a second. Then, without a sound, he pitched slowly backwards and plummeted 30 feet onto the jagged rocks below.

Oblivious to possible witnesses, the wiry Laurie scrambled quickly down to the splayed figure of his former friend. The Englishman was not dead. A thin pink foam smeared his lips. His dazed, unseeing eyes were fixed on the westering sun. He moaned feebly. But the futile whimpering was soon silenced. Laurie's arm rose and fell like some deadly metronome beating out a cadence of death. It did not cease until the Londoner's face was obliterated and his head a bloody pulp.

No twinge of remorse touched Laurie. Quickly he rifled the dead man's pockets and a string of obscenities echoed in the still of the gloaming — for all his boasting, Rose had little in the way of money.

The corpse was the next problem. Flies were already crawling on the shattered head. Other climbers might appear at any minute. Fortunately Rose was a lightweight. Laurie hefted the gruesome burden to a huge granite slab which stood sentinel over Coire-na-Fuhren — the Gully of Fire. Beneath it was a deep crevice, ideal for his purpose. Unceremoniously he bundled the corpse into it and quickly walled up the cavity with stones and moss.

There in the still solitude of the glen he had fashioned a macabre sepulchre for the holiday friend who had boasted too much. Without a backward glance he hurried off down the mountain.

According to the prosecution at his trial, those were the murderous actions of John Watson Laurie on that fateful afternoon of July 15, 1889.

A vain, self-styled dandy, he was selfish in the extreme, conceited and totally unscrupulous. An inveterate liar with a total disregard for others, he displayed all the egomania of the classic psychopath.

That sweltering July was a red-letter month in the calendar of crime. Jack the Ripper had butchered his seventh and last victim and the evil Mrs. Maybury was standing trial for the callous poisoning of her husband.

But the Arran Murder took pride of place with its gory death in the Gully of Fire . . .the mass manhunt for Laurie who brazenly wrote to the newspapers about its inability to capture him . . . the spectacle of eminent medical experts at each others' throats . . . and talk of secret experiments with human skulls.

The relationship between Rose and Laurie had begun innocently enough with a chance meeting on the pleasure steamer Ivanhoe, which plied the popular Clyde Estuary during the summer season. At 25, the swarthy and saturnine Laurie was the black-sheep of a well-to-do Coatbridge family. He had already brushed with the law over the theft of some jewellery which the family had made good. The character of Edwin Rose, on the other hand was without blemish. Slight, with a luxurious moustache, he was still, at 32, a keen athlete. One of an archetypal Victorian family of three brothers and four sisters, he was frank, talkative and cheerful.

But he had one pleasant characteristic which was in the end to prove fatal — he made friends easily.

On the fatal day, Laurie returned alone to the lodgings he had shared with Rose in the small village of Corrie. In the morning he was gone without paying any rent. Gone also were Rose's possessions. Laurie moved on to Rothesay on the neighbouring island of Bute, where his conduct was incredible. Far from fading anonymously away, he strutted proudly among the hansom cabs and gaily dressed promenaders, resplendent in the stylish striped tennis blazer and white serge yachting cap — that once belonged to Edwin Rose.

Meanwhile, search parties combed the mountains and ravines of Arran for days without success. Then, in the weeping grey mist of the evening of August 4 a shepherd glimpsed something pale between some rocks. He rolled them aside and started back in horror. The clawing

He fell backwards on the jagged rocks below

fingers of a human hand stretched out to him, as if grasping for the light.

At midnight the huge silver orb of the moon cast a surreal light as six men gingerly carried a rough wooden box containing the last remains of Edwin Rose on their final journey to the Corrie Hotel. There, two local doctors carried out a post mortem by candle-light and the superstitious locals buried Rose's boots on the sea shore, lest his ghost should return to walk among the living.

By now John Laurie was on the run. But like Peter Manuel some 60 years later, he could not bear to be out of the limelight for long and there was nothing he liked better than to make a fool of the police. As the hue and cry raged up and down the country he wrote to various newspapers.

From Liverpool, he contacted the North British Daily Mail: "I rather smile when I read that my arrest is hourly expected."

In another letter to the Glasgow Herald he denied that he was responsible: "I read so many absurd and mad things in the daily papers that I feel it is my duty to correct some of them . . ."

Eventually he returned to home territory and was spotted outside a railway station at Larkhall, Lanarkshire. After a chase by police and a group of miners he was dragged out of a copse with an open razor in his hand. His throat was partly severed.

"Could you not have granted me the time to do the job properly?" he complained. "I am Laurie. I robbed Rose but did not murder him."

No trial that century had so stirred the public imagination. As John Laurie stepped into the grim, narrow dock at Edinburgh's High Court on November 8, 1889, a crowd of thousands beseiged its doors in Parliament Square.

The circumstantial evidence was heavily weighted against Laurie. But the real battleground of the case was over the cause of death.

Medical experts for the Crown, including Sir Henry Littlejohn, categorically ruled out an accidental fall.

Three other eminent physicians, appearing for the Defence were equally adamant that a fall was the most likely explanation. One of them was Dr. Patrick Watson, surgeon to Queen Victoria in Scotland who had been carrying out experiments with human skulls behind closed doors.

Laurie's counsel, Dean of the Faculty, Mr. J. B. Balker Q.C. brilliantly marshalled the facts in favour of his client. Laurie had no apparent motive. Who would murder for such a meagre return? Who would parade in a dead man's clothes the day after butchering him? The lack of blood proved that death had been instantaneous and not the result of a prolonged battering. Not one article from Rose's body had been directly traced to Laurie.

The consensus of opinion was for "Not Proven". But John Laurie wasn't to escape on what Sir Walter Scott once described as "that bastard verdict."

In sinister candlelight as the hands of the court clock crept towards midnight; the Judge, Lord Kingsburgh, donned the black cap and sentenced him to death.

In the box, Laurie wheeled to face the court and shouted out: "Ladies and gentlemen, I am innocent of the charge."

Nowhere has the rampant hypocrisy of the Victorian era been more apparent than in the uproar which followed the trial. One minute the populace had been baying for his extinction. Now there was an astonishing about turn and self-righteous outcry for mercy, with 138,000 signing a reprieve petition. Two days before the sentence was carried out, Laurie was judged to be insane and was given penal servitude for life instead.

And life was exactly what it meant for Laurie. After 20 endless years his sentence was reviewed but his mental condition was judged to have deteriorated. Decades passed. The Great War came and went. The Wall Street Crash reverberated around the world and Hitler's jackboots were echoing on the Rhine when John Watson Laurie passed peacefully away in his sleep on October 4, 1930.

With him to the grave he took the grisly secret of what really happened on that idyllic summer's afternoon . . .41 years before.

The Hopetoun Quarry Scarecrows

Ominous storm clouds darkened in the west over Midlothian as Billy Higgins helped his small brother John into his threadbare Norfolk suit and the two little boys set off hand-in-hand to meet their dad. Billy was seven, John only four. Shuttling between poorhouses and squalid homes and lodging houses, they had known little but cold, hunger and loneliness ever since their mother had died.

Unloved and unwanted, a strong bond of self-reliance had developed between the sturdy youngsters and local folk in Broxburn and Winchburgh marvelled at the plucky way they faced up to life. Now, washed and scrubbed with tidy new haircuts, it was going to be better — their dad had promised them.

Elizabeth Hynes, a kindly widow, had cared for the boys, though their father Paddy had never contributed a penny. Before they set off that evening, she gave them each a steaming plate of home-made broth to speed them on their way. She was never to see them alive again.

Coated in red dust, Paddy Higgins was finishing off for the day in the brickworks where he laboured, when they hove into view. A dark, stocky man of 38, he had a reputation as a poacher and a heavy drinker.

Albeit he was a popular enough figure in the neighbourhood and there was no hint of tragedy to come as the family threesome set off in the gathering dusk.

Later that evening an unruffled Higgins was to tell a miner friend in the local pub, that he had a stroke of luck. Two friendly ladies that he'd met on the Edinburgh train had agreed to look after the boys.

In the days that followed other strange stories circulated. The boys had gone to relatives in Canada . . . they had been sold for 25/- (£1.25 pence) . . . in his cups Higgins was heard to say that they had "gone to Glory". To the locals it was "the drink talking again" and gradually the memory of the Higgins boys faded into the limbo of the forgotten.

Forgotten that is until a blazing June morning almost two years later — and the gruesome discovery of the Hopetoun Quarry Scarecrows.

The cows were long-since milked and the Sunday church bells rang out over the golden wheat and barley fields near Winchburgh, as ploughman Tam Duncan showed a new grieve round the boundaries of Riddrie Mains Farm. It was a bright and beautiful Sabbath morning — but the horror of it was to remain etched in Tam's memory until the day he died.

As the sun rose higher in the burnished sky, the two men stopped to rest in the shade of the deep, water-filled Hopetoun Quarry. Shrouded in trees, it was shunned by children and adults alike as a sinister and dangerous place. Even the birds were rarely heard to sing in the vicinity.

It was there, floating in the murky, slate-grey water that Tam spotted what he thought was an old scarecrow. The two men went to investigate. It was no scarecrow. The sodden bundle contained two small, decomposing corpses and the brooding waters of Hopetoun Quarry had yielded up a dreadful secret.

A wave of shock, anger and revulsion swept the countryside. When they heard of the dreadful discovery, the Higgins boys and their father Paddy sprang to many peoples' minds. But no-one believed he could be responsible for such a heartless crime.

The word spread that the police would never be able to identify the bodies. A local doctor stated that the remains were unidentifiable.

"In my opinion," he said, "an autopsy would be a waste of time. Decomposition is too far advanced."

But two of the leading pathologists of the day, Professor Harvey Littlejohn and Professor Sydney Smith of Edinburgh University disagreed. Using their scalpels like artists' brushes, they assembled an identikit jigsaw of vital clues which were evenutally to lead Paddy Higgins to the gallows.

Littlejohn and his promising young assistant saw at once that the bodies had been in the water some time. Fully dressed they had been roped together with a window cord, which could lead to only one conclusion. It was a case of cold-blooded murder. But the police were completely at a loss until identification was established.

He thought it was an old scarecrow floating on the water

At first sight the pathetic remains on the scrubbed tables of Linlithgow mortuary promised little. The bodies had almost totally transformed into adipocere — a condition which converts normally fluid human fat into a solid white substance not unlike mutton suet, when a body has been immersed in water for a lengthy period.

In both bodies adipocere was almost complete and it was possible to estimate that they had been in the quarry for 18 months to two years — no longer. There was no external indication of sex but by piecing together the remains of microscopic glandular structures, Smith was able to prove that the bodies were male. Direct measurement gave the heights as 3'7½" and 3'2" — the average heights of boys of six to seven and four years old.

A vital piece of evidence emerged from an inspection of the hair remaining on the scalps. It could be proved that both victims had had haircuts just before they were murdered.

Absolutely crucial was the evidence found in the contents of the stomachs, miraculously preserved by adipocere. There were definite traces of home-made scotch broth, the Higgins' boys fateful last meal. With incredible accuracy, it was possible to estimate that the broth had been eaten about an hour before death and the obvious conclusion was that the boys had lived locally and knew their killer well.

The net soon closed on Paddy Higgins when the police learned that his two young sons had disappeared mysteriously in November 1911.

Higgins had served for seven years with the Scottish Rifles in India. He had been an excellent soldier and a first-class signaller. When he returned to Winchburgh he married a local girl but when she suddenly died in 1910 he'd started to drink heavily and had neglected his sons.

In January 1911 they were taken to the poorhouse and when Higgins refused to pay 8/- (40 pence) a week from his 24/- (£1.20 pence) a week wage for their upkeep, he was jailed for two months. On his release he collected the boys and took them to the kindly Mrs. Hynes in Broxburn. At the time of their death, he was once more being threatened with prosecution for failing to maintain his sons.

Circumstantial evidence piled up as witness after witness came forward with the conflicting stories he had given for the boys' disappearance. Eventually he was arrested at dead of night at a Broxburn lodging house only a few days after the bodies had been found.

Poker-faced and without the slightest trace of emotion or concern he rose from his bed and said: "That's me they want, I believe." When asked about his sons, he said he didn't know where they were.

At his trial at the High Court in Edinburgh three months later he was described as a "cold, callous, morally depraved creature" who had brutally murdered his sons simply because they were a financial burden and a nuisance. A special plea of insanity was entered. There was conflicting evidence that he suffered epileptic fits due to a head injury. A certain degree of mental enfeeblement was obvious. It was said that he had no idea of right and wrong and that his emotional nature was degraded.

A deep silence fell in court as the jury announced a unanimous verdict of guilty — with a recommendation for mercy. Higgins sprang to attention as the Judge, Lord Johnston, donned the black cap and sentenced him to death with the fateful last words — "And this is pronounced for doom." As he was led below to the cells there was a jaunty nod and a wink for friends and relatives on the public benches.

On the morning of October 2, 1913, the condemned man ate his last meal and took communion in his small cell next door to the gallows. Again he stood to attention as his arms were pinioned and the white hood slipped over his head. A minister intoned: "Into Thy hands O Lord I commend thy spirit." Higgins responded with his last words on earth: "Lord receive my spirit," just as the trap was sprung.

There was a festive air among the crowd that gathered on Calton Hill above the prison yard. Though nothing was visible, some clambered on the monumental canons to satisfy their morbid curiosity. As the hour of eight boomed out over the city, the grim, black, flag, signalling that the execution had been carried out, rose slowly above the prison. The crowds gradually dispersed, many of them on their way to Musselburgh Races.

At the foot of the Nelson Monument a blind fiddler was playing "The Lost Chord."

Footnote: Pathologist Sydney Smith (later to be Knighted), was so impressed with the perfect example of adipocere in the bodies that he turned bodysnatcher and comandeered large portions of the corpses for Edinburgh University's Medical School. This led to an embarrassing moment when he travelled by train from Linlithgow to Edinburgh with his prizes wrapped in brown paper in the luggage rack. The eminent physician had to make a hurried and furtive exit when the parcels started to reek abominably in the hot summer weather.

Case of the Jealous Mother

In a dazzle of scarlet, black, white and emerald green, the prancing pierots and harlequins slashed the stage of the Aberdeen Pavilion with harsh primary colours. As they pirouetted and whirled, the older performers held little interest for the slight, thin-lipped woman in the fourth row of the stalls. Clad still in her sensible brown overcoat, her normally reserved, almost severe features were unusually relaxed. Her eyes were fixed on the subdued pastel dresses of the small girls in the chorus.

There, second from the right, was her daughter Jeannie — in her mother's eyes, the true star of the seaside summer show. The special dancing lessons, scrimped and saved for, had been worth every penny. How radiant Jeannie looked. How gracefully she danced. How much more lovely than the others. There was only one discordant note. The heavy-handed tinkling of the piano. The clumsy pianist was ruining the performance.

A slight frown darkened Jean Donald's brow. A dreadful memory stirred. A memory of faltering piano notes, a simple scale, repeated and repeated. A memory too terrible to contemplate.

Earlier that day, the innocent sound of a child practising on the piano had transformed Jean Donald — regular attender at Salvation Army mothers' meetings, model housewife, doting mother and staunch churchgoer — into a cold-blooded killer. It had triggered one of the most appalling murders ever committed in Aberdeen.

During the trial, witnesses and members of the public, broke down and wept but through it all the dark haired housewife in the dock maintained an inscrutable mask of douce respectability. Slight of stature with delicate features, the only incongruous note was the large workman-like hands, clasped quietly in her lap.

That Jean Donald was guilty, there is no doubt. But what deep-seated pressures caused the Jekyll and Hyde transformation from demure housewife to pitiless killer? Was she responsible for her actions? Did she in fact have any memory of her homicidal behaviour on the afternoon of April 20, 1934 . . .

It was a typical Thursday lunchtime at the working class tenement in Urquhart Street. In the ground floor flat at number 61, Jean Donald welcomed her barber husband in the perfunctory manner born of a long and uneventful married life.

As he settled to his meagre lunch, he cast a jaundiced eye at the colourful array of rayon, silk, chiffon and satin displayed on the alcove bed. For several years now, every spare penny had been devoted to his precocious daughter's dancing dresses but Jim Donald knew better than to criticise. Matters relating to little Jeannie's "career" were sacrosanct.

A more immediate worry was the sound of a piano filtering down from the flat upstairs. Jim Donald sighed inwardly. The Priestlys, their

"My bairn, my bairn," she screamed

neighbours, had recently bought a piano for their daughter Helen, a pert, vivacious child of ten, only a year older than Jeannie. And his wife had taken it as a personal insult. For the thousandth time Jim wondered if his wife's attitude towards their daughter was quite normal. A mother's ambition was one thing, an all consuming obsession was another.

Jean Donald had not spoken to Mrs. Priestly for some time now. She gave no reason but Jim Donald thought he understood. Looked at dispassionately there was little to choose between the little Priestly girl and his own daughter in terms of talent, looks and personality. In her obsessive way Jean Donald saw Helen Priestly as a threat. At times Jim had caught a strange hard look in his wife's eyes as she watched the Priestly girl skip through the close.

With the advent of the piano, which gave the girl upstairs an unfair advantage in his wife's eyes, life had become impossible. Rarely a day passed without some reference to it. Now as the faltering scales from upstairs continued, Jean Donald's hackles rose again.

"You'll hae to tell them to wheesht with that piano," she said, "before it drives me mad."

With a weary nod the barber put on his raincoat and left for the long afternoon's labour in his shop. In later years he was often to recall the prophetic ring to his wife's last words to him that fateful lunchtime.

It was now 1.30 p.m. and upstairs the Priestlys too had finished lunch. Before Helen returned to school her mother sent her on an errand to the store just around the corner. Muffled snugly in her overcoat, with a bright yellow tammy on her head, the little girl ran off down the stairs. She was never to return.

Eventually Mrs. Priestly became worried at Helen's non-arrival back and ran to tell her husband. The frantic parents and neighbours scoured the area and the police were informed. As the hue and cry developed with anxious voices echoing in the close and heavy footsteps clattering on the stairs, the door of the Donald home remained resolutely closed. Outside a steady downpour cast a dismal pall.

Just after five o'clock Jean Donald and her daughter, on their way to the performance at the Pavilion, bumped into a neighbour.

"Have you heard about wee Helen Priestly?" asked Mrs. Donald. "I almost collapsed when I was told." Then clutching her daughter's hand, she hurried off.

As dusk fell and streetlights glimmered on the cold, grey granite of the city, the search continued. It was unavailing and eventually Jim Priestly, who had aged five years in five hours, called a halt until five a.m. the next morning.

Soon after the search restarted, loud shouts shattered the quiet pre-dawn in Urquhart Street. Wrenching herself from restraining arms Mrs. Priestly rushed downstairs. A small bundle had been found in the recess under the stairs. Half hidden in the gloom, it looked like a small sack of potatoes. Helen Priestly could see two small feet protruding from the mouth of a sack.

"My bairn, my bairn," she screamed as she flung herself down beside the body of her daughter.

When the police arrived, they found the body cold. The sack was clean and dry as was the lobby. Since it had been raining heavily throughout the night, it appeared unlikely that the sack and its grisly burden had been carried in from outside. There were no footprints in the mud of the back green.

The state of the body caused even the most hardened police officers to shy away. Death had been caused by strangulation. It was not the bruised windpipe that appalled the officers however. It was the brutal lacerations of the small girl's genitals. The injuries were such that those investigating soon decided that they had been inflicted as a red-herring. The motive for the killing had not been a sexual one.

One strange and important clue was a cinder found clenched between the girl's upper and lower lips. There were others in her hair and the net began to close inexorably on Jean Donald. When she was eventually charged with the crime, five days after the murder, her only words were: "I did not do that." During the interim she had not paid one visit of condolence to her neighbour and her contribution towards a wreath for the dead girl had been one shilling. (Five pence.)

Inside Jean Donald's home the police found important evidence. Though the box in which the Donalds put their ashes had disappeared, hairs which matched the dead girl's were found in the grate. Fibres discovered in the Donald home were found to match the fibres on the sack in which the body was found. More damning still were the washcloths in Jean Donald's sink. In a triumph of scientific detection they were found to contain a very unusual strain of coliform baccilus which was also found in the dead girl's underclothes.

Such was the hatred of Jean Donald in Aberdeen there is little doubt that in days of rougher justice she would have been lynched. Local prejudice forced the trial to Edinburgh.

One of the first witnesses was Mrs. Priestly, who broke down several times as she recounted the last few moments she had spent with her daughter. Women members of the jury hid their eyes but Jean Donald, dressed in black, maintained her inflexible composure throughout.

Her advocate pointed out that there was absolutely no motive. The crime was utterly senseless. There was no hint of malice. No woman, herself the mother of a little girl, would have been capable of such an attack.

The judge, Lord Aitchieson, indicated that proof of motive was not necessary. He said the Law did not require mathematical certainty — only reasonable certainty of guilt. The jury took only a few minutes to record a verdict of guilty. As she was sentenced to death, Jean Donald's composure broke for the first time. Moaning "Oh no . . . oh no . . ." she collapsed in a faint.

There was joy bordering on hysteria in Aberdeen. The worthy townsfolk were even more delighted when it was announced that the

£3000 cost of the trial would not be added to their rates.

Their vengeful satisfaction was short-lived however. A week before she was due to be hanged at Aberdeen Prison, Jean Donald was reprieved. The sentence was commuted to one of penal servitude for life.

From Bible Class to Bullets

Mid-day on Sunday and the genteel West End of Glasgow lay becalmed in the late summer sun. Shoes polished, faces scrubbed, shorts and summer dresses neatly pressed, a Sunday School class of youngsters waited expectantly for their teacher.

He was a strange, young, fair-haired fellow and they did not know quite how to take him. On the one hand he could be bossy and sarcastic. On the other, he made the Bible stories more exciting than any other teacher. Mr. Finlay really lived the part. Perhaps he was an actor.

Edwin Finlay was no actor however. The children waited in vain on that August Sunday in 1952. They were never to see the slim teacher with the dark, intense, eyes again. Soon Edwin, model son of devoted parents, former pupil at Glasgow High School, keen tennis club member, and bank clerk, would be infamous — as a bank robber and killer.

In the aftermath of one of the most futile bloodbaths in the annals of Glasgow crime, one policeman lay dead, another was fighting for his life and Edwin Finlay himself had fallen — a bullet from his own gun lodged in his brain.

Edwin was only 18 when he died. He wrote willing all his worldly possessions, including Rusty, his much-loved cocker spaniel to Ann Frier, a girl who had rejected him. But the reasons for his incredible Jekyll and Hyde transformation from bland bank clerk to berserk killer, went with him to his grave.

Interested in sport and a leading light in the army cadet corps, Edwin was not a brilliant scholar. When he left school he joined the British Linen Bank as a trainee bank clerk. His employer was later to say: "He seemed a pleasant sort of boy." But on the Saturday of August 30 the facade of normality was irretrievably broken.

From the bank Edwin phoned Ann Frier, the attractive 17-year-old schoolgirl he had worshipped from afar and talked to occasionally, and tried to arrange a date. She refused. Then the thwarted Edwin was sent on an errand to the head office.

He never returned.

Bank staff discovered that almost £1000 was missing from the emergency fund. Though it was hard to swallow the only logical conclusion was that Edwin Finlay was responsible.

The hue and cry was on — but behind the anonymous and ordinary exterior Edwin had planned his crime with military precision. Before the police had even been informed, he was winging his way from Renfrew Airport to Dublin. Strangely, he felt no fear, no guilt, no apprehension . . . only a wild exultation. He'd finally done it. He'd shown them. He was no mouse, he was a man of action. Even Ann would realise now that he was someone to be reckoned with. In one dramatic stride the meek bank clerk had been transformed into an amalgam of Al Capone and a commando officer — roles he had often played before in the Walter Mitty dream world of his mind.

There was one important difference now however — fantasy had become irreversible fact.

In his best tweed suit and raincoat, in the Humphrey Bogart style, the runaway bank clerk nonchalantly signed in at one of Dublin's best hotels, posing as Lieutenant Edwin Finlay. He said he was on leave from the Korean War and no questions were asked when he purchased two hand guns and 500 rounds of ammunition at a gunsmith's in the city.

Four days later he flew back to Glasgow. It was Thursday September 4.

What triggered Edwin's fatal return to Scotland remains a mystery. He may have realised that capture was inevitable. Perhaps, racked with guilt, he wanted to make peace with the invalid father he was devoted to. Maybe, in typically psychopathic fashion, he was goaded by the lack of publicity. Possibly it was one last gesture towards the girl he was obsessed by.

When he arrived in Glasgow he telephoned Ann Frier's home. Her mother answered that Ann was not at home. Then she telephoned the police and told them that Finlay regularly waited at the junction of Hyndland Road and Great Western Road in the evenings in the hope of having a few words with Ann on her way home.

To the officers in the city's Marine Division it seemed routine. There could not be much to fear from "a schoolboy bank robber." Two plain clothes constables, John MacLeod and Tom MacDonald, were sent out to see if anything emerged from the tip-off.

The scenario then took on a nightmarish quality.

It was just before eight o'clock as the two policemen approached the rendezvous point. As if on cue Edwin Finlay appeared round the corner walking towards them on the opposite side of the street. The officers had no reason to expect trouble. They were not to know that the slim bank clerk had transformed himself into a walking arsenal, bristling with no fewer than three hand guns and more ammunition that he could ever use in a flamboyant bandolier round his waist.

The policemen crossed the road towards the pallid Finlay. MacLeod, a 31-year-old married man with a small son, spoke first. "Excuse me," he said. "I'm a police officer. Are you . . ."

He got no further. The youngster sprang back pulling two guns from his bulging raincoat pockets. "Stand back," he shouted, then there was a flurry of four or five loud cracks.

The bank clerk opened fire . . .

The first shot took MacLeod full in the chest. He fell without sound and lay quite still. As Constable MacDonald, a former paratrooper, dived forward, a bullet shattered his arm. Still he came on, until another shot ripped into his groin. Clutching his wounds he staggered onto the pavement and collapsed close to the motionless form of his friend and partner.

For a few split seconds the tableau remained frozen. Finlay seemed mesmerised by the enormity of what he had done. Then from a lane just down the road a uniformed policeman appeared. He was Constable Charles Hill, whose beat covered the Hyndland Road area and he had come to investigate what sounded like a car backfiring. He rapidly re-evaluated the situation when Finlay loosed off a shot in his direction.

Hill, armed only with a baton, was not deterred. He had recognised one of his colleagues prone on the ground. Showing remarkable courage he charged straight towards the youth with the guns.

Finlay dashed down a nearby lane — a narrow cul de sac with high stone walls between tall houses. As the policeman made to follow, the bank clerk wheeled and fired a staccatto burst. The bullets whined harmlessly over Hill's head and knowing his quarry was now trapped in a dead-end he dived for cover behind a wall at the entry.

"You've had it," yelled Hill. "Throw down the gun."

"I'll take you with me if I go," screamed Finlay, true to his gangster fantasies until the end.

Then there was a short lull, punctuated by sporadic shots. By now dusk was falling and police cars and men were pouring into the area. Crowds had to be held back in Hyndland Road.

Eventually a group of officers infiltrated a back garden behind Finlay and suddenly burst through the garden wall door into the lane. The fugitive ran a few steps. Then, as if realising the odds against him were hopeless, he came to a halt. Slowly . . . almost resignedly . . . he raised a gun to his head and pulled the trigger. Edwin Finlay's fevered imagination was at last stilled.

Constable MacLeod died in hospital later the same evening. Constable MacDonald however survived after several days on the critical list. Both were awarded the British Empire Medal.

Later it emerged that before the final rendezvous Finlay had visited a cafe haunt of schoolboy friends. One had seen him twirling a revolver on his finger, cowboy style. He'd asked Finlay what he was doing with such an amazingly convincing replica. The reply, considered a joke at the time, now had a sinisterly prophetic ring.

"They'll never take me alive," he'd bragged. "I'll save the last bullet for myself."

The Killer in the Camel Hair Coat

Thick, freezing fog entombed the city streets on the south side of Glasgow. It was December 10, 1945, a black and bitter night in the austere days just after the Second World War.

Traffic was at a standstill. Trains, if at all, were running late. At the entry to Pollokshields East, a railway station on the suburban Cathcart Line, only a few minutes from the city centre, two down-at-heel street musicians were playing Christmas Carols. Takings had been meagre. Chilled to the marrow, they were about to call it a day, when a solitary figure emerged from the station entry. It was a slim young man with an American-style snap-brimmed hat pulled well down and a camel-hair coat, with padded shoulders. He looked like a toff.

One of the buskers moved forward, cap outstretched, to bar his way but the young man brushed hurriedly by, tossing a handful of silver in his wake. In all there was well over £1, an unexpected windfall, but there was little of the Christmas spirit in the manner the money was given.

"Who does he think he is?" muttered one musician to his mate, as the man in the hat was swallowed by the fog.

"Some kind of flipping big shot, I suppose," replied his partner.

At that stage they could not realise the macabre accuracy of the comment.

A few minutes earlier, in the small station-master's office, the entire staff at the enshrouded station had been huddling round the meagre warmth of the small coal fire. William Wright was the 42-year-old porter/clerk, Annie Withers a 36-year-old clerkess and Robert Gough, a slightly-built 15-year-old, had only recently left school to become a boy porter.

Like a scene from a gangster film, the door to the platform suddenly swung open. The astonished staff were confronted by a man they had never seen before. He was wearing a camel-hair coat and the type of hat not often seen on the streets of Glasgow. The clothes were unusual but it was not that which drew their eyes. Clenched in the man's right fist, pointing straight at them, was a gun.

For a few brief seconds the tableau remained frozen. No-one spoke. Then Annie Withers screamed. It seemed to galvanise the ashen-faced gunman into action. He took a deep breath, then the gun barked twice.

The clerkess fell to her knees, clutching her side. Twice more the gun exploded and she collapsed backwards, her blood seeping onto the worn floorboards. Attempting to shield her, young Bobby Gough's arm had been shattered by a bullet which riccocheted on into his abdomen. Bill Wright fell too, as the homicidal stranger sprayed the small office with bullets.

There was no panic in the killer's actions. Quickly he rifled the cash drawer and vanished into the night. The haul was a mere £4-3-8d. (£4.18p).

Bill Wright who had escaped with a graze on his side, phoned the nearest signal box. Then, as an overdue train pulled into the station, he staggered on to the platform. In keeping with the nightmarish quality of events so far, the train guard thought it was a practical joke, blew his whistle and hopped back aboard the already moving train.

Help came with the arrival of the police a few minutes later. But it was too late for Annie Withers. She died in an ambulance on the way to hospital. Two days later, the heroic schoolboy porter, Bobby Gough died too.

The police were baffled. There were some fingerprints on the cash drawer but there was no trace in the criminal files in Scotland or England. They were looking for a slim, ginger-haired young man . . . with no criminal record. Despite intensive checks, it was like looking for a needle in a haystack. Eventually the Pollokshields murder slipped into the limbo of the forgotten.

Ten months passed. Then, in early October 1946, police, acting on a tip-off that "a man on the south side had a luger pistol", arrived at the door of railway fireman Charles Templeman Brown's home in Brisbane Street, Cathcart. Charlie lived with his widowed mother and he was away at work so a message was left asking him to call at the local police station.

When the 21-year-old fireman did arrive back, early the next morning his mother passed on the message. "I know why they were here," was his only remark.

He washed and shaved, then walked out of the house, ignoring the breakfast his mother had set on the table.

"Charlie's not himself today", she thought, for her son's manners were usually beyond reproach. A quiet, considerate young man, he worked hard, did not smoke or drink and made good money, a good proportion of which went towards the family.

Open and generous, Charlie Brown was always smartly dressed and well-groomed. With his fresh complexion and neatly parted ginger hair, he was the apple of his mother's eye and the envy of her friends and neighbours . . . the perfect "boy-next-door."

The only flaw, if any, was Charlie's fads and fancies. At one stage, when he was younger, Mrs. Brown had worried a little. Charlie was such a hero-worshipper. And some of his heroes left a lot to be desired.

At one stage he had been keen on gangsters. He'd gone to see the Al Capone film "Scarface", at least five times. Pictures of Stalin and Hitler had appeared on his bedroom walls. Now however, his tastes had modified. The heroes he idolised today were a bit more normal — Joe Loss the bandleader and an American crooner called Frank Sinatra. Aping the singer, he'd taken to wearing snap-brimmed soft hats and multi-coloured bow ties.

The clerkess collapsed . . . blood dripping on to the floorboards

"I suppose it's all just part of growing up," thought Mrs. Brown, as she ruefully cleared away her son's congealed breakfast plate.

Two hours later the hard-working widow woman's world disintegrated, when her son, the archetypal boy-next-door, admitted that he was the heartless killer of Pollokshields East.

At 9.50 a.m. Charles Templeman Brown approached a policeman in nearby Spean Street and asked: "Will you phone the Central police for me?"

"Why?" asked the policeman.

"I did a murder," said Brown. "The Pollokshields job."

Then he handed the astonished officer a 1918 Luger and a box of ammunition.

By coincidence, Brown's trial at Glasgow High Court started on December 10, 1946 — a year to the day after the shootings. It soon became clear that the question was not whether he had been the gunman. But whether or not he had been sane when he committed the crimes.

In court the pale-faced Brown was imperturbable. The fact that he faced the death penalty did not disturb him in the least. From Barlinnie Prison he wrote a chatty letter to a friend which finished with the P.S. "My favourite tune at the moment (fanfare of trumpets) . . . Day by Day, sung of course by Frankie. Tell Bell when you see him. Bing is KAPUT."

In the box, his mother said that over the last two years her son had become moody and irritable. He suffered from headaches and tended to plunge quickly from moods of elation to depression. The main line of the defence became clear when a specialist in mental and nervous diseases confirmed that in his opinion Brown had been suffering from dementia praecox when he committed the crimes. One of the symptoms was that the sufferer developed a world of fantasy, taking refuge in daydreams and craving public attention.

Then came the crunch question. "Would you be prepared to certify that Brown was insane?" The doctor's reply encapsulated the controversial and sometimes contradictory aspects of psychiatric evidence.

"Medically, yes," came the answer. "Legally, no."

Other medical experts recounted how Brown had told them he regarded himself as a "Dillinger Youth" and a "Sinatra Youth."

"What does that mean?" asked the Judge, Lord Carmont.

A doctor explained that Dillinger was an infamous gangster and that Sinatra was "an American who appears in films."

"Is Sinatra a real person?" queried the judge.

"Yes, my lord."

"And Dillinger is a real person?"

"Yes, my lord."

After an absence of an hour the jury found Charles Templeman Brown guilty of murder. He remained impassive as Lord Carmont donned the sinister black cap and sentenced him to death. The execution date was fixed for January 3 1947. But Brown did not keep his date with the hangman. Four days before sentence was due to be carried out, he was repreived and sentenced to life imprisonment.

A note to friends, written long before in his railwayman's notebook read: "I'm not sorry for anything I did, only for the things I didn't do."

Fate however had not finished with Charles Brown. He was released from prison in 1957 and in 1960, while driving with a girlfriend near Dunblane, he swerved off the road and crashed into a wall. Charles Templeman Brown was killed instantly. The Jekyll and Hyde of Pollokshields had died as he wanted to live — sensationally.

Incredibly, for the third time, the fatal date was December 10.

The Twisted Dr. Cream

The flaring gas jet of the tall street lamp guttered in a sudden April shower. A notorious beacon in the night life of Victorian London, it was a well-known haunt of prostitutes. The "frail flowers" of the night and the predatory men-about-town who sought their favours were lured to it like moths in the night.

On the fateful midnight of April 11, 1892, however, the illicit trade in mercenary sex was at a standstill. The theatres and music halls had long-since closed. The glittering crowds of tall silk hatted toffs and extravagently dressed women had melted away with the last stylish carriage.

The two young women stood hesitantly beneath the lamp, clutching their bonnets in the boisterous wind. To the experienced eye, Alice Marsh and Emma Shrivell were obvious "beginners", in their squalid trade. Emma was only 18. Alice 21. Country girls, they had been lured from their homes near Brighton by the promise of the bright lights and a fortune to be made — in return for virtue.

Sickened by the brutality of the so-called "gentlemen of quality" who were the customers, Emma decided that this night was to be her last as a streetwalker. Tired and chilled she made to leave but Alice's hand stilled her. Out of the darkness at the end of the street a hansomcab appeared.

Silhouetted in the gloom inside was a man in a tall silk hat. A black gloved hand beckoned them closer. Emma giggled involuntarily and Alice nudged her in warning although she could hardly restrain the urge to smile herself. For beneath the tall hat she was looking into a pair of absurdly eager, yet grotesquely squinting eyes.

Stifling their mirth the girls accepted the stranger's proposition and climbed into the cab. As they trotted through the darkened streets, he told them that his name was Fred. Emma again giggled uncontrollably.

But the brittle laughter would have died on her lips if she had known that the midnight trip in "the toff's" hansom cab was the last cab ride she would ever take. A journey that would end in long hours of agony and a horrific and lingering death.

For the man beside her was Dr. Thomas Neill Cream — one of the most perverted psychopaths ever to emerge from the nineteenth century streets of Glasgow. He was a multiple killer, whose depraved sexual desires and the methods he used to satisfy them, placed him on the pedestal of infamy alongside Jack the Ripper.

The girls took the bizarre customer to their seamy lodgings in Stamford Street. He was a strange one and no mistake. His demands were insatiable and he offered them more money to wash down some pink capsules with the champagne he'd provided. He said the capsules were from France — "to refresh you in the lists of love."

Ten minutes after he had left, an unearthly scream of agony woke everyone in the lodging house. Alice Marsh lay writhing in the hall outside her room. She was drenched in sweat, her body wracked with violent spasms. Another tortured shreik came from beneath the bed in the girls' room. Emma Shrivell had crawled there as if to flee the dreadful pain. Her nightgown was in tatters and she had drawn blood with the spasmodic clawing of her own nails.

Dazed and sickened the landlady rushed from the room and sent her husband for a doctor. She tried to administer an emetic of mustard and water. It was all in vain. Alice was fortunate to die on her way to hospital, begging for one last look at her illegitimate baby boy. Emma was to linger on for six hours in unfathomable pain, which no medicine could alleviate.

No-one knew this better than the evil Dr. Cream. For those who swallowed his "pink pills for pale prostitutes" — death was a blessed release.

The full death list of Dr. Cream will never be accurately known. That he was involved in at least eight deaths has been definitely established. There is little doubt that there were many more.

He was born on May 27, 1850 at 61 Wellington Lane, in the heart of Glasgow. The eldest of five sons, his family emigrated to Canada and Thomas entered McGill University to study medicine in 1872. He was a brilliant scholar and graduated with merit in 1876. Despite his looks he fancied himself as a ladies' man and it was this more than anything that led him into the picaresque career which could have been dismissed as a black farce — if it hadn't been so lethal.

In 1874 he almost killed his sweetheart performing an abortion and was married to her at shotgun point. In 1875 his wife died and he claimed a 1000 dollar settlement before she was cold in her grave. In 1877 he gained double honours at the Royal College of Physicians and Surgeons, after a stay in Edinburgh. In 1878 a chambermaid in Ontario was asphyxiated with chloroform. She was pregnant and the doctor was suspected but there was no proof. In 1880 he was charged with the death of a Canadian girl during an abortion in Chicago. Again there was no

A black-gloved hand beckoned them close

proof. In 1881 a woman patient died after taking some of his medicine. Once again he escaped charges.

Incredibly, the good doctor was still allowed to practise medicine and he advertised a cure for epilepsy. Sufferer Daniel Stott, a railway agent in the Middle West, sent his pretty young wife for the medicine. It's hard to fathom the fatal attraction wielded by the boss-eyed Dr. Cream . . . but like so many before she soon became his mistress.

She calmly watched her 61-year-old husband swallow the lethal strychnine pills that Cream had prescribed. He died in agony 20 minutes later and it was attributed to an epileptic seizure. Cream and his mistress would have escaped scot-free, but for the monumental egotism of the psychopath, which led Cream to accuse a chemist he didn't like, of blundering with the dead man's prescription. Because of the complaint the body was exhumed and the homicidal doctor was sentenced to life imprisonment.

But the world had not heard the last of the doctor. In 1887 his father died leaving him a fortune of 16,000 dollars. Possibly this helped him gain release some four years later, and the doctor decided on a holiday in England, to celebrate. On October 1, 1891, the unlikely killer with the face of Ben Turpin and the mind of a viper, stepped ashore at Liverpool.

Packed neatly in his luggage were enough strychnine capsules to poison every man woman and child who had sailed with him on board SS Teutonic and he plunged eagerly into the squalid twilight world of London's nightlife, to make use of them.

On October 13, Ellen Donsworth, a 19-year-old "unfortunate" fell writhing in agony in the street. Five days later, Matilda Clover, another young streetwalker, died in the same way. The deaths would have passed unnoticed but for an anonymous letter to the coroner offering information on the poisoning of Clover, if the government would pay £300,000.

That poison had been involved was news to the authorities. Matilda had been a chronic alcoholic and the cause of death had been diagnosed as acute delirium tremens. Now her body was exhumed and found to contain enough strychnine to kill ten able-bodied men. Only one man living could have known about the poison — and that was the killer who had written to the coroner. At this stage there was nothing to connect Cream with the letter but later it was to play a vital part in the evidence against him.

Well satisfied with his holiday jaunt to London, the maniacal doctor recrossed the Atlantic, but soon he was to return in search of further human prey.

The violent and convulsive deaths of Alice March and Emma Shrivell soon followed, along with further anonymous letters. Then Louisa Harvey, the luckiest young streetwalker in London, contacted Scotland Yard. She'd had a narrow escape from Cream. Meeting him at the St. James Music Hall she had spent the night with him at a Soho hotel and he'd promised her some pills to cure a skin complaint.

They met again at night and Louisa pretended to swallow the pink capsules. The man she called "Dr. Fred" did not linger to view his handiwork. He made an excuse and hurried off. Police technicians soon established that the pills were lethal.

Like many psychopaths Neill Cream talked too much and to the wrong people. Police became suspicious and began to shadow him. Eventually he was arrested and charged with murder. His trial at the Old Bailey began on October 17, 1892.

Confident of acquittal after an inspired speech by his counsel, the crazed doctor was seen to sing and dance in his cell but the verdict of guilty was a foregone conclusion. Much to his own surprise Dr. Cream found himself with an early morning appointment with the hangman. He took the fateful short walk to the permanent execution shed at Newgate Prison with quiet dignity.

He had no words to say concerning his victims or his guilt as the black flag fluttered to the masthead and a great cheer rose from the thousands gathered outside the prison in the chill grey morning.

That Cream was guilty, there is no doubt. But the society which turned a blind eye to the squalor and vice that seethed just below the surface and allowed the deranged doctor — with his horrendous track record — to walk abroad, was guiltier still.

In the backwaters of Lambeth, life is no longer as cheap as the favours of a fallen woman. Some say however, that when the light is right and midnight strikes, the ghost of the boss-eyed doctor from Glasgow still stalks the mean streets in search of one last "frail flower" to add to his collection.

The Schoolboy Killer

Some say the Devil was on hand when Donald Merrett was born in New Zealand in 1908. Outwardly he was a normal boy — big for his years with a strangely adult air — but normal none the less. Genetic chance however, made him a freak as surely as one physically deformed, for he was a psychopath and the ingredient of conscience was non-existent in his make up. Cold, callous and ruthlessly selfish, he carried an invisible mark of Cain, that meant death and destruction to those who loved him most.

In retrospect, his father John Merrett made an inspired decision when he deserted the family when Donald was still a toddler. The mother, Bertha, was cultured, musical and intelligent and she had a private income which enabled her to provide the best of education for young Donald. Mother and son travelled half-way round the globe then she enrolled the precocious boy at Edinburgh University. When they took up residence in a rented flat at Buckingham Terrace in 1925, she was 56 years old and in the prime of life — but she only had a few short months to live.

Long, tedious hours of study were not for Donald Merrett. He did however spend a great deal of time mastering the intricacies of the "Palais Glide" in the city's sleazier dance halls, where he was rumoured to be a millionaire's son. It was not surprising that his wallet always bulged for, at the age of 16, he had added forgery to his string of many talents, copying his mother's signature on a series of stolen cheques.

He splashed money on dance hall hostesses, bought a second-hand motorcycle, and far more ominous — a snub-nosed Japanese pistol.

Bertha Merrett however, was careful and meticulous with her accounts. Her son's raffish progress was on a collision course with disaster. No-one knew his forgeries would be discovered shortly better than he. What a tiresome fuss there would be. The callous, psychopathic, mind of Donald Merrett was soon made up. His mother was a nuisance . . . she was in the way . . . she was going to cause a rumpus. She would be better dead.

After breakfast one morning Donald Merrett rose from his chintz arm chair beside the fire, with the small pistol he now kept at all times in his possession, in his hand. He crossed the room to stand behind his mother who was bent over a ledger at her desk.

Without looking up she said: "Go away Donald and don't annoy me." They were the last words she was ever to speak to her son. No flicker of emotion moved in his dark eyes, no spark of filial affection. Coldly he raised the snub-nosed gun, levelled it as his mother's ear, and pulled the trigger.

Bertha Merrett screamed just once before she collapsed on the floor. The expressionless Donald calmly wiped the gun and tossed it by her side, then he ran to the kitchen and told the maid: "Rita, my mother has just shot herself."

For two weeks Bertha struggled to survive in the locked ward of a mental hospital, reserved for suicide attempts. In a lucid moment she told her sister: "I was sitting writing and Donald was standing beside me. Suddenly a bang went off in my head, like a pistol."

Three days later she was dead, hopefully unaware that her beloved son had killed her.

When Merrett's forgeries came to light he was charged with matricide but the police bungled their investigations, the medical evidence was conflicting and in the end, probably due more to Merrett's extreme youth and the unspeakable nature of the crime, than anything else he escaped with the Scottish verdict of "Not Proven." John Donald Merrett was free once more in an unsuspecting society.

Adopting the name of Chesney, he went to stay in England with a Mary Brennar, Lady Menzies, an old friend of his mother.

"If it's the last thing I do, I'll repay you for your kindness," he told her. And he was quick to keep his word, breaking her heart by eloping to

Scotland with her 17-year-old daughter Vera and marrying her at the Glasgow Registrars.

Initially it didn't seem such a bad match. When Donald came of age, he inherited a £50,000 fortune from his grandfather. At last the high-stakes world of fast cars, beautiful women, playboys and gamblers was his. He bought a 20 room mansion, a Bentley and a private aeroplane. His sleek yacht became a common sight in the Mediterannean, where he indulged his Walter Mitty dreams by dabbling in gun-running and smuggling. Playing the part to the hilt, he grew a thick, black beard and wore a gold ear-ring.

For the deadpan professional gamblers of the Riviera, roaring-boy Merrett was easy game. Soon the fortune dwindled but not before he made an £8,500 settlement on Vera, which he was later, in impecunious times, to describe as "a mental aberration". The endowment, which reverted to him upon her death, proved in fact to be her death warrant.

Commissioned in the Royal Navy during the war, he was known as "Crasher" after piling up no fewer than three motor torpedo boats. (MTB's). Without a scruple in his body, he was also totally without fear, wading single-handed through the surf towards the advancing Germans at Tobruk, spraying them with machine-gun fire, in the best Errol Flynn tradition.

Later in post-war Germany his reputation gained almost mythical proportions when he stole three lorry loads of army rifles, ferried them across the border to East German black marketeers — and got away with it. It seemed a fitting climax to his military career when he stole the palatial Koch limousine which had once belonged to Admiral Doenitz and drove to Paris for a weekend with his current mistress.

Back in Civvy Street, times were hard and Donald Merrett was rushing pell-mell towards disaster. He was a marked man with Interpol and as his smuggling activities were becoming more and more curtailed, his thoughts inevitably turned to the £8,500 he had settled on his now estranged wife, Vera.

She had by now become an alcoholic and was running a home for retired gentlefolk in London with her mother. In January 1954, Donald travelled to England to see her and took her on a pub crawl to establish that they were still the best of friends.

Returning to Germany, he told his stunning blonde mistress of the moment, Sonia Winnikes: "Pack your bag, we're going on holiday to Amsterdam." She obeyed without question. For a man with all the sexual finesse of an orang-outang, Donald Merrett was never short of female company. The holiday however, was interrupted. He would be gone for only one night. A business deal had come up.

Shaving off his beard and removing his ear-ring, he combed his hair back, donned a pair of horn-rimmed glasses and, walking with a limp, he boarded the evening flight for London with a forged passport in a different name.

He carried her into the adjoining bathroom

Later that February night, his breath plumed white as he kept a lonely vigil in the bitter shadows just across the road from his wife's home in Montpellier Road. One by one the lights in the gloomy, red-brick, Victorian house flicked off until the only illumination came from his wife's upstairs bedroom.

With surprising agility for a man of his massive, 22 stone bulk, Merrett vaulted the garden fence and made straight for the french windows. The faulty catch, as he suspected, had not yet been mended. Inside the dogs, who knew him well, nuzzled him without a sound. He tip-toed up the stairs and through the slightly musty darkness towards the ribbon of light beneath his wife's bedroom door.

Vera, sitting at her dressing table, was startled by his sudden appearance, but her eyes, already glazed with drink, lit up when she saw he'd brought a present — two bottles of duty-free gin. Powerless in the baffling progression of alcoholism, the two green bottles took on the mantle of priceless treasure. Skin and bones now, the hair lack-lustre, the face raddled and haggard, her hands shook so, she could hardly pour. As far as the psychopathically omnipotent Merrett was concerned, getting rid of her was doing the world a favour.

An hour of affable chatter, at which Donald Merrett had no equal, interspersed with frequent libations from the gin bottle, was enough. Vera suddenly passed out. With surprising gentleness for one who bulked so large, Merrett carried her silently into the adjoining bathroom, filled the bath and carefully lowered the unconscious woman into the tepid water. She did not stir, there were no desperate last throes. Poor Vera seemed to welcome death. Cocooned in gin, she slept on undisturbed, as her last hold on life eddied away.

Exulting, Merrett hurriedly retraced his steps. It had gone off like clockwork. For once he had come up with a winning hand. But Fate had one more bad card to deal the man who was known in gambling circles from Berlin to Monte Carlo, as "Unlucky Merrett."

He was back on the ground floor when the bird-like figure of Lady Menzies, Vera's mother, barred his way. A murderous rage exploded in the big man's mind. With one huge hand closed savagely over the old lady's mouth, he clubbed down on the frail grey head with a heavy coffee pot.

This killing could never be explained away but as he strode away through the dark streets of London on the morning of February 10, 1952, John Donald Merrett was still immortal in his own mind. After all, had he not escaped the hangman once before — for the murder of his own mother more than 30 years ago.

By the time he'd returned to Germany, however, the confidence had evaporated. Scotland Yard were not slow to put two and two together. Once more he was on the run from Interpol. Even his mistress now rejected him. Tired, alone and strangely forlorn without his bucaneering beard, he took one last taxi ride through the dark streets of Cologne and out into the country. There, in a copse beneath the stars, he placed the barrel of his Colt .45 in his mouth and calmly snuffed out his own life, with the same detached proficiency he had shown to others.

Bloody Jigsaw of Gardenholme Linn

On September 29, 1935, Susan Johnson, a young holidaymaker from Edinburgh, set off for a walk near Moffat in Dumfriesshire. On a bridge over Gardenholme Linn, a fast flowing boulder-strewn stream, that tumbles into the nearby River Annan, she stopped to admire the view. Glancing into the depths of the ravine below, she spotted something which had an uncanny resemblance to a human arm.

White-faced, she ran to the police. At first sceptical, they investigated, and soon the grim-faced officers were involved in the most harrowing search of their lives.

By mid-afternoon, four grisly bundles containing parts of legs, arms, breasts, thighs, heads and one trunk, had been discovered. As more and more fragments came to light the exhausted searchers gave up trying to estimate how many bodies had been butchered. Of one thing they were certain, however. They were dealing with a particularly apalling case of murder.

The first two forensic experts on the scene were Professor John Glaister of Glasgow University and Dr. Gilbert Miller, a pathologist at Edinburgh University. Working in trying conditions in the small mortuary at a cemetery near the bridge, their first problem was to decide how many bodies were involved in the carnage. The conclusion was that there were not more than two. A local joiner fashioned a pair of rough and ready, coffin-like boxes which were labelled "Body No. 1" and "Body No. 2".

A far more complex problem was establishing the sex of the remains, for the bodies had been severely mutilated to hinder identification. From both of the heads, the tissues of the face had been cut away, including the noses, lips, ears, eyes and skin. Some teeth had been extracted after death and the internal and external organs of sex had been completely removed.

From the 70 pieces recovered, two bodies were meticulously reconstructed, complete except for one trunk and a few other small parts. The eventual conclusion was that they were women. The cold-blooded butcher responsible had indulged himself in a gruesome marathon of dissection and it was patently obvious that whoever was responsible possessed detailed medical and anatomical knowledge.

Meanwhile, a Dr. Buck Ruxton, reported that his wife and a maid were missing from home in Lancaster. Dr. Ruxton was an Indian. His name was originally Bukhtyar Hakim. He qualified at the universities of Bombay and London and eventually settled in the north of England where he ran a large and successful practise and was well thought of by his patients.

The 36-year-old doctor met Isabella Ruxton — they were known as man and wife, though, in fact, they were never married — in 1927. From the start it was a stormy and passionate relationship, for the highly emotional physician was morbidly jealous and possessive. There were furious outbursts and dire threats were often made. Police had been called several times to deal with disturbances.

The three Ruxton children, aged two, four and six, were doted on by their young nursemaid, Mary Jane Rogerson. She was a cheerful and friendly girl of 20. Devoted to her parents, she spent all her free time with them and if she ever went away on holiday, or for any other reason, she religiously wrote them a letter every day. But in mid-September she disappeared . . . and there were no loving letters.

When the parents enquired, the rattled doctor gave several conflicting reasons for Mary's absence. First he told them she had gone away on a tour to Edinburgh with his wife. Then he came up with the unlikely tale that Mrs. Ruxton had taken their daughter away to have an illegal abortion. Naturally, the distraught couple went to the police.

Prior to this, Ruxton himself had angrily approached the police. By sheer coincidence, they had been questioning one of his house cleaners about another case in Morecambe.

"What the hell do the police mean by inquiring into my affairs?" the doctor wanted to know. In a highly emotional state, he went on to pour out all his woes.

Pointing to a deep gash in his hand, he said that he had injured it opening a can — the result, he explained, of having to fend for himself, "while my wife is away." He said he had not seen her since she had gone to Blackpool on September 14 — and he invited the astonished police to come and search his house. This was an invitation which they ignored.

A few days later he was back at the police station. This time he loudly claimed that his name was being unjustly linked with the human remains the newspapers reported had been found at Moffat.

"All this damned nonsense is ruining my practise," he said. "Can nothing be done to stop all this talk?"

Cleaners who worked at the Ruxton house were spoken to and told of unusual incidents which had not appeared suspicious at the time. Numerous blood-smeared articles had been seen in the house. Carpets had been removed. A bath was stained a dirty yellow colour. One woman had been ordered to burn a blood-stained suit of clothes and a carpet in the back yard. Staircase walls had been stripped and redecorated and there were further bloodstains on the curtains.

By now the police were highly suspicious but they needed a connecting link between the remains at Moffat and the missing women.

She spotted what appeared to be a human arm

This was provided by the wrappings round some of the human fragments. A blouse with a patch under one arm and a pair of rompers had been used and they were both identified by Mary Rogerson's parents.

A special "slip" edition of the Sunday Graphic, containing a picture of two beauty queens with the partial headline ". . . AMBE'S CARNIVAL QUEEN CROWNED." was also part of the grisly wrappings. The newspaper had only been distributed in the Lancaster area.

Dr. Ruxton was formally cautioned and charged with the murder of Mary Rogerson.

When the case moved south the Scottish forensic team moved with it. In the hushed Ruxton house in Dalton Square, the doctors worked behind closed doors and drawn blinds, as crowds of morbid sightseers jostled on the pavements outside. In the cold, unheated, rooms, with the outlandish Oriental decor and sky-blue ceilings with silver stars, they toiled deep into the night in the golden light of hastily rigged gas flares.

There were many incriminating traces of blood, but Professor Glaister was not satisfied. He arranged for his most famous reconstruction. A "doll's house" replica had been suggested but the gimlet-eyed pathologist was never one for half-measures. Much in the style of an eccentric American millionaire, he ordered huge sections of the house to be transported to Glasgow, lock, stock and barrel. Then, in the laboratories of Glasgow University, portions of several rooms and the entire bathroom were meticulously rebuilt. Many more human bloodstains were discovered.

Something highly sinister had obviously happened in the house but the bodies had still to be identified. It was here that the evidence of the pathologists was of paramount importance. Without it Ruxton would probably have escaped the hangman. Many precedents were set in the case, which is rightly considered "a classic" in medico-legal circles.

A portion of skin had been removed from "Body 1", where 'Mary Rogerson was known to have a disfiguring birthmark. The same was true on the left foot of "Body 2", just where Mrs. Ruxton had had a septic bunion scar. Photographs of both women were obtained for a new technique. Experts produced life-size blow-ups of the heads and when photographs of the skulls found at Moffat were superimposed, they were found to match exactly.

Ruxton's trial began before Mr. Justice Singleton at Manchester on March 2, 1936. The prosecution's theory was, that in a fit of insane jealousy, the doctor had gone berserk and murdered his wife, then the maid, because she had witnessed the first killing.

During questioning the doctor had already admitted: "We were the kind of people who could not live with each other and could not live without each other."

He had also quoted a French proverb — "Who loves most, chastises most."

The small coloured doctor cut a sorry and insignificant figure in the box. Pathetically nervous, he was found guilty. Later an appeal was dismissed and he was executed on May 9.

Dead Men DO Tell Tales

The first rays of the autumn sun were slowly warming the heather on Bolfracks Hill. A wisp of breakfast smoke curled from the chimney of the small white cottage. Perched high on the hill overlooking Loch Tay, the McIntyre family, who lived there had one of the most spectacular views in Scotland on their front door step. The only drawback was the loneliness and isolation. It was a fatal characteristic, which led to bloody murder.

Mr. McIntyre was head shepherd on the mountainous Tombuie Estate in Perthshire. His son Archie was also an estate worker, his daughter Mary, a typist and another daughter, Annie, was off on holiday as their 47-year-old mother, Catherine, bustled about her kitchen on that bright September morning.

Deep in the emerald green of the bracken there was a slight movement. A kestrel soared from cover into the clear morning air. There was a scent of menace and danger on the quiet hillside. From a cunningly concealed lair among the fronds, pitiless eyes registered every movement at Tower Cottage. For two long days without food or water, Polish deserter Stanislaw Myszka had crouched unseen, with murder on his mind.

A slight, sallow, 23-year-old, with thin, predatory features, he had camoflaged himself in old overalls. With a sawn-off shotgun in easy reach he'd noted every departure and arrival. He knew when each member of the family left for work. He knew when they returned. He knew when the lone postman paid his call. And he knew above all, that there was little likelihood of visitors.

Like an animal in his lair, the little Pole with the incongruous bullneck, constantly re-read a grimy letter that had come from his estranged wife in Paris. It told him that the two young sons that he'd been separated from by the war, were to be sent back to a poorhouse in Poland, unless he could join them in France with some money. Though the war was long over by the autumn of 1947, he could not approach the authorities, since he was a deserter two times over and was a wanted man in Poland, Germany and France. Stanislaw Myszka was a desperate man. He had to find some money — and he was prepared to commit murder to get it. Today his sinister vigil was over. Now was the time to strike.

His last action was a strange one for a man intent on violence. Perhaps it was a throwback to his military training, but before he strode, shotgun in hand to the cottage door, he carefully shaved with a dry razor and tossed the blunted blade into the heather. It was a fatal blunder which eventually led him to an appointment with Pierpont the hangman.

At about eight o'clock young Archie McIntyre was the last to wave goodbye to his mother. He was also the first to return to the cottage at tea time. The family's small Cairn terrier rushed to greet him, barking furiously. The cottage door was locked but Archie was not surprised. His mother had promised to help light the fires for a deerstalking party at Bolfracks House. Archie settled down on the doorstep with a newspaper that was still in the letterbox.

The first pangs of alarm came with the arrival of gamekeeper and neighbour, Duncan McKerracher. Where was Archie's mother? She had promised to have tea with Mrs. McKerracher and hadn't turned up.

Something was far wrong and Archie knew it. He ran for a ladder and clambered through a window into the kitchen where he'd left his mother 10 hours before. Apart from his own nervous breathing the dim room was as silent as a tomb. The first thing that jarred was the kitchen dishes. His mother was a neat and methodical woman, yet they were still lying unwashed on the table. Desperately alarmed now the young man raced to his mother's and sisters' bedrooms. The beds were unmade. More ominous still, pen, ink and an unfinished letter lay on the kitchen table. Catherine McIntyre must have been disturbed while she was writing it.

The frantic son next tried the stoutly built door of his own bedroom. It was locked. He needed an axe to smash his way in. There, draped in a blood-stained sheet on the bed, was the body of his mother. Bed clothes and furniture were strewn about the room. The gentle lady of Bolfracks Hill had put up a desperate struggle, before being bludgeoned to death.

It became apparent that the murderer had known there was a considerable amount of money in the cottage. Mr. McIntyre in fact held the £85 pay-roll for the estate workers and it had disappeared from its secret hiding place in a chest of drawers.

The horrific discovery sparked off a nationwide manhunt. The killer had worn gloves and there were no fingerprints but painstaking teams of police and scythe-weilding ghillies and gamekeepers started a foot by foot search. Before long they discovered the flattened bracken from which Myszka had made his murderous reconnaisance . . . and several vital clues. The most important find was a safety razor blade with a few blond hairs sticking to it. There was also a shotgun with a bloodstained butt and the pieces of a Perth-Aberfeldy railway ticket, of the type issued to servicemen in uniform only.

The ticket was a vital lead, for down below, close to the shores of Loch Tay was Taymouth Castle. Once the stately home of the Duke of Breadalbane, it was now being used as a resettlement centre for 800 Polish soldiers, who had elected to stay on in Scotland after the war rather than return to their own communist-dominated homeland. They

He needed an axe to smash his way in

were constantly on the move between Perth and Aberfeldy by train.

As police intensified their enquiries, the net began to close on Stanislaw Myszka. A local taxi driver reported a strange fare, a foreigner with dirty shoes who had not spoken a word on the 35 mile journey to Perth. The man wore brown kid gloves, which he had never removed and he was racked by a bad cold. Though he looked as if he had been sleeping rough he had paid from a thick wad of banknotes.

Meanwhile a gardener in Old Meldrum, Aberdeenshire, recognised a description of the shotgun used in the murder. He had loaned just such a gun to a local grieve but it had disappeared and when police investigated, they found that Myszka had been odd-jobbing at the farm at the time. More damning evidence came from a local girl who had married a Polish serviceman. Myszka had visited them several times, and she was suspicious. When he left before the murder, he was broke. When he returned he took the couple on a spending spree in Peterhead.

Odder still had been his guilty reaction when a newspaper report of the murder hunt had been read out to him.

"His face lit up like fire," the woman told the police. "And when I said, 'I wonder who could have killed that poor woman?', I was shocked when he replied, 'I did what was done at the farm but I did not kill the woman.'

A dragnet was flung around Peterhead and two policemen were making a hut by hut search at a disused airfield at Longside when a figure broke from a doorway. Myszka was making a last frantic bid for freedom across the fields but he was quickly brought down and overpowered. Later at Peterhead the police had difficulty keeping a vengeful, booing crowd at bay as the pallid fugitive was led away on his last journey to Perth Prison.

Scotland's leading pathologist, Professor John Glaister, a man who repeatedly proved that dead men DO tell tales, had been called in. He believed that all criminals left some sort of "visiting card" at the scene of every crime. So it was to prove with the rusty razor blade found among the bracken on Bolfracks Hill.

No-one was better qualified than Glaister to interpret the evidence of a few stubby blond hairs still stuck to the thin wafer of steel. From his earliest days as a young doctor he had made a special study of hair. He was a world-recognised authority on the subject. Though identification by means of hair is not as foolproof as fingerprints, it nonetheless carries a great deal of weight in the courtroom.

Glaister asked for some samples of the prisoner's beard. Under the microscope samples from the razor blade, alongside the new shavings proved to have the same gross and detailed characteristics. At the trial Professor Glaister stated that "the hairs were so similar as to be consistent with a common source of origin."

This forensic evidence was of vital importance and it left the four women and 11 men of the jury in no doubt as to their verdict. Myszka had pled Not Guilty and entered a special defence that he was insane and not responsible for his actions at the time of the crime.

Throughout the trial the little Pole in the shabby greatcoat listened impassively, his face a sallow mask as doctors and psychiatrists confirmed that they were in no doubt as to his sanity. The only ray of hope came when one of them did agree that, "In extreme cases, lack of food and exposure might reduce a man to a state where he was not responsible for his actions."

The jury was not impressed. They retired for only 20 minutes before returning a verdict of Guilty. Lord Sorn donned the black cap and pronounced the death sentence. In the dock Myszka betrayed the first signs of emotion when he flushed and ducked his head.

In the grey drizzle of an early morning three weeks later, he walked silently between two prison warders to meet the hangman. When asked if he had any last statement to make, he merely shook his head.

Psychic Murder?

On the well-tended greensward, among the carved tombstones of Scotland's Kings, on the sacred island of Iona, a tiny memorial often goes unnoticed. In the open pages of a small book in white marble, are embossed the words:

N.E.F. DIED 19th NOVEMBER, 1929. Aged 33 years.

The initials stand for Norah Emily Farnario. And behind the brief inscription lies one of the most macabre sudden deaths in Scottish history.

Half a century ago Iona, serene and mystic isle of bleached white sands and azure seas, was totally isolated from mainland civilisation. There were no roads or public transport. No electricity, no running water, no daily papers, no radio, no telephones. To get there involved a sea voyage from Oban to Mull followed by a long and tortuous journey over rutted tracks to the ferry from Fionnphort, across the one and a half mile Sound of Iona.

The journey, which now takes a bare six hours from Glasgow, then took upwards of two days. It was like travelling to a foreign land.

In the autumn of 1928, Norah Farnario arrived in Iona from her home in London. Seeking peace and serenity, she had heard "The Call" of the island.

An attractive, fragile looking woman, she parted her raven-black hair in two heavy, chain-like plaits. Somewhat eccentric, given to wearing multi-coloured, hand-woven clothes, she spent most of her time writing poetry and studying folklore. Deep dark and intense eyes were Norah's most striking feature.

In London she had dabbled in spiritualism, theosophy, thought-reading and faith healing. She had become a member of the Alpha and Omega occult group — one of the many that sprung up when the "dark powers" were in vogue in the earlier part of the century, due mainly to the influence of Aliester "The Beast" Crowley.

Norah had also been an associate of Mrs. Mathers, a well-known medium and sister of the philosopher Henri Bergson. Mrs. Mathers' husband, Samuel Liddell Mathers, was a leading light of another group of occultists, called, The Golden Dawn. It is worth noting that the alleged penalty for breaking the Golden Dawn's oaths of silence, secrecy and loyalty, involved being subjected to a "current of will" which would cause the offender "to fall dead or paralysed, as if blasted by lightning."

The attraction of the small island (3½ miles by 1½ miles) to someone seeking loftier spiritual planes, is an obvious one. The landing place of St. Columba is steeped in religious history. Iona Abbey, lovingly rebuilt by the Iona Community, in memory of the Irish monk who brought Christianity to Scotland, dominates the island. In St. Columba's Bay at the South End, huge mounds of stones rise on the beach like giant molehills and no-one can explain them. Beneath Dun I, the highest hill, are the remains of a long-dead hermit's cell. At the North End, the blood of the devout, slain by Viking raiders, once soaked the pristine sand on the "White Strand of the Monks."

The natural reticence of the West Highlanders did not disturb Norah Farnario. Daughter of an Italian academic and an English gentlewoman, she boarded on an island croft. Her hosts were somewhat disturbed by her, however. There was a strange, faraway look in her eyes when she spoke of visions, of spiritual healing and messages from the spirit world. She kept two oil lamps glowing in her room throughout the night but this did not prevent the ornate silver jewellery she constantly wore, mysteriously turning black.

One spot on Iona held a particular fascination for Norah. Surrounded by steep rocks and treacherous marshes, it was the site of an ancient village, thought to be pre-Christian. It could be reached only by foot and there the spirits of the dead were said to roam. As the bitter autumn winds swept through the bracken and crusty marsh grasses, Norah spent many solitary hours in this desolate spot. She seemed impervious to cold.

As time went by, the mysterious lady from London's behaviour became even stranger. There were signs of increased anxiety. The repose she once had, disappeared. Her speech became more rapid . . . disjointed . . . sometimes incoherent. She told her hosts not to be alarmed if she happened to go into a trance, even if it lasted up to a week. If that happened she was not to be disturbed and under no circumstances was a doctor to be called.

A creature of the night, Norah seldom rose early, but one morning this routine was broken. She was up and about just before dawn in a state of near panic. Her dark hair, usually so immaculate, was lank and unkempt about her strangely pallid face.

She had to leave the island immediately, she said. There was no time to lose. She talked in disjointed sentences. Hysteria was not far away. In her ramblings she mentioned "a rudderless ship that went across the sky" and "messages from the world beyond". The distraught and anguished woman spent the morning hurriedly packing her belongings. She paid no

The macabre condition of the body horrified the searchers

heed when she was told there was no means of leaving the island because it was Sunday and the ferry didn't run on the Sabbath.

The fact that she was marooned did not get through to her until she stood, surrounded by her baggage, ready to leave. For some time she gazed across the stormy Sound to Mull as if willing a boat to appear. Then her shoulders slumped in utter dejection.

She locked herself in her room for several hours and when she reappeared she seemed to have aged years. Gone was the distress and in its place an air of total resignation. She talked rationally enough before going off to bed.

The customary knock on the door the following morning brought no response. Norah Farnario had vanished in the night. Neatly arranged by the bedside were her clothes and jewellery. When she had not returned by noon a search of the rocky inlets and barren moors got under way. By the premature end of the short, dark, November day, no trace had been found. The ensuing night was moonlit and bitterly cold. Searchers were out again at dawn. Eventually in an isolated area of peat bogs and brackish streams, some two miles from the village, the barking of a collie drew two crofters to a gruesome scene.

Spreadeagled in the heather was the body of Norah Farnario. It was a shocking and nerve-shattering discovery — but what horrified the searchers more, was the macabre condition of the body.

She was naked apart from a long black cloak decorated with occult insignia and a blackened silver chain around her neck. Her face had frozen in a rictus of terror. Her toes and the balls of her feet were torn and lacerated, though the skin of the heels was intact. She had obviously been running full-tilt to escape from something.

Clenched, claw-like in one hand was a long steel knife. The searchers had to forcibly prise her fingers apart to retrieve it. With it she had gouged the rough outline of a cross in the peaty turf. On this her body lay, as if in one last desperate supplication for divine mercy or protection.

The "Call" of the island had led Norah Farnario closer to Hell than Heaven.

Foul play was ruled out. A doctor who had never encountered circumstances remotely like it before, gave "heart failure" as the cause of death.

In the weeks that followed there were reports of blue lights being seen in the vicinity of where the body was found. Other unsubstantiated rumours involved a "man in a cloak" and a sighting of Norah on the moors the day that she disappeared. But no further light was shed on the strange end of the eccentric lady from the south.

The world of the occult was in ferment and there were accusations of "psychic murder". There was no doubt in the mind of Dion Fortune, a leading figure in occult circles. She was adamant that Norah Farnario had died in a premeditated psychic attack.

She pointed out that the body had been badly scratched. That Norah had been associated with Mrs. Mathers. That Mrs. Mathers had been linked with known cases of "Astral Attacks" and the victims of these attacks always bore scratch marks.

Black magic . . . heart failure . . . exposure? We will never know. The secret of Norah Farnario's last hours died with her. Now all that remains is the memorial in the island's famed Reilig Odhrain burial ground. And a small cairn built by the crofters, on the spot where they found her on the moorland of death.